weblinks

You don't need a computer to use this book. But, for readers who do have access to the Internet, the book provides links to recommended websites which offer additional information and resources on the subject.

You will find weblinks boxes like this on some pages of the book.

weblinks

For more engineering careers advice, go to www.waylinks.co.uk/ series/soyouwant/engineering

waylinks.co.uk

To help you find the recommended websites easily and quickly, weblinks are provided on our own website, **waylinks.co.uk.** These take you straight to the relevant websites and save you typing in the Internet address yourself.

Internet safety

↗ Never give out personal details, which include: your name, address, school, telephone number, email address, password and mobile number.

↗ Do not respond to messages which make you feel uncomfortable – tell an adult.

↗ Do not arrange to meet in person someone you have met on the Internet.

↗ Never send your picture or anything else to an online friend without a parent's or teacher's permission.

↗ If you see anything that worries you, tell an adult.

A note to adults
Internet use by children should be supervised. We recommend that you install filtering software which blocks unsuitable material.

Website content

The weblinks for this book are checked and updated regularly. However, because of the nature of the Internet, the content of a website may change at any time, or a website may close down without notice. While the Publishers regret any inconvenience this may cause readers, they cannot be responsible for the content of any website other than their own.

HODDER
Wayland

So You Want to Work in
Engineering?

Margaret McAlpine

HODDER
Wayland

an imprint of Hodder Children's Books

First published in 2005 by Hodder Wayland,
an imprint of Hodder Children's Books

© Hodder Wayland 2005

Editor: Patience Coster
Inside design: Peta Morey
Cover design: Hodder Wayland

British Library Cataloguing Publication Data

McAlpine, Margaret
So you want to work in engineering?
1. Engineering - Vocational guidance - Juvenile literature
I. Title
620' . 0023

ISBN 0 7502 4580 8

Printed in China

Hodder Children's Books
A division of Hodder Headline Limited
338 Euston Road, London NW1 3BH

Picture Acknowledgements. The publishers would like to thank the following for
allowing their pictures to be reproduced in this publication:
Angela Hampton Family Life Picture Library 46, 50; Bettmann/Corbis 53; Bill
Varie/Corbis 10, 30; Bob Krist/Corbis 54; Bob Rowan/Progressive Image/Corbis 57;
Brownie Harris/Corbis 8, 40, 56, 59; Charles O'Rear/Corbis 11, 31; Colin
Cuthbert/Science Photo Library 51; Eric Hausman/Corbis 52; FK Photo/Corbis 41;
Freelance Consulting Services Pty Inc./Corbis 20; Gabe Palmer/Corbis 37; George
Disario/Corbis 43; Hekimian Julien/Corbis Sygma 48; Jacques Langevin/Corbis
Sygma 24; Jean Miele/Corbis 17; Jeffrey L. Rotman/Corbis 49; Jim Sugar/Corbis 7;
John Madere/Corbis 35 (*middle*); Keren Su/Corbis 25; Lester Lefkowitz/Corbis 13,
16, 29; Lucidio Studio Inc./Corbis 15; M. L. Sinibaldi/Corbis 33; Orban
Theirry/Corbis Sygma 35 (*bottom*); Paul A. Souders/Corbis 4; Paul Steel/Corbis 23;
Peter Barrett/Corbis 55; Pete Saloutos/Corbis 5; Philip Gould/Corbis 42; Ralf-Finn
Hestoft/Corbis 6; Reuters/Corbis 27 (*middle*); Richard Hamilton Smith/Corbis 45;
Rick Gayle/Corbis 27 (*bottom*); Roger Ball/Corbis 36, 38, 58; Roger
Ressmeyer/Corbis 9, 14, 28, 47; Stephen Frink/Corbis 44; Steve Crise/Corbis 22;
Ted Horowitz/Corbis 32, 39; Tom and Dee McCarthy/Corbis 12; William
Taufic/Corbis 18, 19, 20.

Note: Photographs illustrating the 'day in the life of' pages are posed by models

Contents

Words in **bold** can be found in the glossary.

Aeronautical/Aerospace Engineer

What is an aeronautical/aerospace engineer?

Aeronautical and aerospace engineers make things fly. They plan, design, build and maintain aircraft, missiles and spacecraft. Aeronautical engineering is a traditional form of engineering which includes the design and manufacture of conventional **civilian** and military aircraft that fly in the atmosphere (the band of gases that surrounds the earth).

Aerospace engineering includes aeronautical engineering, but it also focuses on space travel and **automated flight control** systems, such as missiles and satellites. Aerospace engineers can be found working in motor sport and **automotive** manufacturing too. Here they usually specialize in vehicle design, helping to make cars less wind resistant. They also work in boat and ship design, where they use their knowledge of the flow of air and water and how this affects the movement of structures.

Aeronautical engineers have used studies of birds' flight patterns to help improve aircraft design.

Experiments with flight

Humans have always been fascinated by the idea of flight. In 1486, the artist, sculptor and engineer, Leonardo da Vinci, began studying birds to find out how they flew. He went on to design a number of different flying machines based on his research, but none of these was successfully constructed.

The most famous aeronautical engineers were two brothers named Wilbur and Orville Wright. In 1903, the Wright brothers carried out the first successful powered flight in a heavier than air machine with a pilot on board. Afterwards they set up an aircraft factory. This marked the beginning of the aeronautical industry.

Today air travel is the best way to cross the world quickly and safely.

Since that time, all successful aeroplanes have incorporated the basic design elements of the brothers' aircraft, known as the Wright Flyer. The way the brothers worked set the pattern for research and development in the aeronautical engineering industry. They carried out carefully planned tests, collected data (information) which they examined and analyzed carefully and used to make changes to their designs.

Main tasks of an aeronautical/aerospace engineer

Aeronautical and aerospace engineers need to have a very good understanding of aerodynamics (the study of how objects move in the air).

Aerospace engineers usually specialize in a particular area of work. The main areas are research and development, design, model making, production and maintenance.

- Research and development – this involves trying to solve problems, for example, caused by weather conditions or the altitude (height) of a flight, which affect the safety and smooth running of aircraft. It includes making **modifications** to aircraft and their engines as new materials are invented and technology moves forward.
- Design – this involves improving the design of aircraft to make them travel faster and more safely while also making them more fuel efficient and cheaper to build. Design also involves drawing up plans for new aircraft.

Aeronautical and aerospace engineers oversee the maintenance work that is carried out regularly by mechanics to make sure that aircraft are safe to fly.

Good points and bad points

'Supervising the maintenance side of the aerospace industry is a great job. I like to feel I'm using my knowledge and qualifications in a practical way.'

'My job carries a lot of responsibility, so it is quite stressful. I cannot afford to make a mistake.'

- Models – this includes making models that are tested thoroughly to make sure a new design of aircraft can do what it is supposed to do. Working on models means many problems can be identified before large amounts of money are spent.
- Production – this involves working on the construction of aircraft. Engineers work in aircraft factories, supervising the manufacture and making sure it is of a high standard.
- Maintenance – this involves checking all aircraft frequently and thoroughly for safety reasons. In this way, weaknesses or problems can be identified before they become a danger to passengers and crew. Engineers generally supervise a team of technicians who carry out the maintenance work.

Aerospace engineers use models such as these to identify problems that might occur in a real aircraft.

Some engineers choose to specialize in a specific type of vehicle, such as fixed-wing aircraft or rockets. Others become experts in one area of work, such as guidance systems, used to control the direction of missiles, or propulsion, the means by which an object is pushed forward.

Skills needed to be an aeronautical/aerospace engineer

Creativity
Aerospace engineers are pushing back boundaries of science all the time. They need to think creatively and use their imaginations to visualize how something might be in the future.

Scientific knowledge
Aeronautical/aerospace engineers need to have an excellent knowledge of physics, chemistry and maths.

An eye for detail
Although engineers may work on huge projects, they still need to carry out very detailed and precise work.

Awareness of safety needs
Safety is a major issue in air travel because accidents in the air are very serious. If passengers feel unsafe on a plane they will choose another method of transport next time they travel. Engineers need to make sure that the highest safety standards are in place in their designs.

This engineer is working on a jet engine. Aeronautical engineers need to have advanced technical knowledge and skill.

Teamwork
Aerospace projects can be enormous and involve a large number of people. They all need to share their ideas and work well together.

Communication skills
Aerospace engineers working on large projects need to be able to express themselves clearly both in speech and writing.

Designing aircraft to cope with the rigours of space travel poses a challenge for aerospace engineers.

fact file

Aeronautical/aerospace engineers need a high level of scientific and technical knowledge. They will usually have taken a degree, followed by a period of further study and practical work in order to gain a professional qualification. People wanting to become engineers can take a modern apprenticeship, which involves work and study. Qualifications gained as a modern apprentice can lead to a place on a degree course.

Computer skills

All engineering jobs involve the use of computers. There are special software programmes designed specifically for the aeronautical industry, particularly in the area of design.

Language skills

The development and building of new aircraft is enormously expensive. Countries often work together and share the costs. For example, the International Space Station project is a global partnership involving sixteen nations. This type of international cooperation is likely to become more common, which means that aerospace engineers who speak a foreign language will be in great demand.

A day in the life of an aeronautical engineer

Martin Jones

Martin works at an aerospace manufacturing research centre. He is currently working on an international project involving a number of different countries in the development of a new passenger plane.

9.00 am   I arrive at work and check my emails. Working on a huge international programme means we rely on electronic communication to keep in touch.

9.30 am   At present most of my working life is spent at my computer, which is where I am at the moment. The main part of my job involves event **simulation**. Using computers I am able to create an on-screen version of the project, from which I can predict whether a proposal we have received to undertake work from a company would meet our requirements at a price we could afford. The simulation also shows any problems that might arise.

10.30 am   I look at proposals to design and **manufacture** the wings of the plane. I break down the information I am given so that it can be entered into the computer.

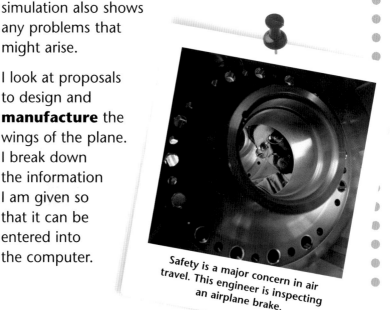

Safety is a major concern in air travel. This engineer is inspecting an airplane brake.

International projects such as Airbus bring together aerospace engineers from all over the world.

2.00 pm   For once I am not working on-screen. Instead I am researching the information needed for a future event simulation. This involves phoning different departments and asking them to send me figures and dates.

4.00 pm   I work on a presentation I am to give at an international meeting in a month's time. **Delegates** from different countries will be there and I shall talk to them about the proposals we have simulated on-screen and how they fit in with projected budgets and timetables.

6.30 pm   After a day in the office, I switch off my computer and join some colleagues for a game of squash.

Chemical Engineer

What is a chemical engineer?

Chemical engineers develop new products in laboratories. They make small quantities of the substance and carry out tests to make sure it is safe. They also need to ensure it does the job it is supposed to do and can be produced at a reasonable cost.

Chemistry is the study of substances, what they are made from and how they react when they are put together. Chemical engineers solve practical problems by using chemistry to change materials in a chemical process. Chemical engineering combines chemistry, maths and physics in a practical way.

Everything that is manufactured, or made by people, involves chemical engineering. For example, fabric, paper, soap and shampoo manufacturing all involve processing of some kind and chemical engineering.

Chemical engineers develop new products in laboratories, carrying out tests to make sure they are safe.

The wonders of science

Believe it or not, plastic bottles and polar fleece jackets are made from the same material! Chemical engineers have developed a process that melts down used plastic bottles and draws the plastic into a fine yarn that can be used to make cold weather clothes.

Chemical engineers need to supervise production so that all runs smoothly. Here an engineer turns a valve on factory machinery to regulate pressure.

If the product passes the tests, chemical engineers turn their attention to producing it in larger amounts. They often use computer models to prepare for this. In this way, they can simulate the manufacturing process. The simulation helps them to see some of the problems that may develop when they produce the real thing.

Eventually, the new product is manufactured and, at this point, the responsibility of chemical engineers changes. Now they must make sure that production runs smoothly, problems are solved, and the quality of the final product is satisfactory.

weblinks

For more information about a career in chemical engineering, go to www.waylinks.co.uk/series/soyouwant/engineering

Main tasks of a chemical engineer

Chemical engineers work in many different areas, using their knowledge and skills to improve life on the planet.

- Food production – chemical engineers develop fertilizers that enrich the soil and give plants the goodness they need to grow well. In this way, they help to increase food production across the world.
- Medical developments – by using special processes, chemical engineers can take small amounts of substances, such as **antibiotics**, and increase them several thousand times. In this way, they can help lower the cost of medicines. This helps people in poorer countries, where there is less money to spend on healthcare than in richer countries.

Chemical engineers work to improve the environment. This engineer is examining a coal 'paste' being developed as a clean alternative to traditional coal.

Good points and bad points

'There are great opportunities for chemical engineers, including the chance to travel with the job. Young chemical engineers who are good at their work are often given opportunities to manage projects early in their careers.'

'Chemical engineering projects often involve a great deal of money, and managing them can be stressful.'

Chemical engineers work to develop artificial organs and body parts, such as eyes, hearts, kidneys, muscles and skin. These medical developments give people with diseased organs a greatly increased chance of survival. Artificial organs need to be made from materials that are not rejected by the human body. Chemical engineers have an important part to play in the development of such materials.

- Improving the **environment** – the work of chemical engineers has provided ways of clearing up waste and pollution. Lead-free petrol and reduced sulphur diesel fuel are results of chemical engineering.
- Development of **synthetics** – synthetic fabrics, such as nylon and polyester and the synthetic rubber found in trainers, bicycles and in-line skates are the results of chemical engineering research and development. Today, **plastic** is found and used everywhere. It is so common that no one thinks much about it. The first plastic, called Bakelite, was developed by chemical engineers.

The synthetic rubber used in trainers was developed by chemical engineers. Synthetic materials are generally hard-wearing and cheap to produce.

Skills needed to be a chemical engineer

Although chemical engineers work in a wide range of different jobs, they all need to have some similar qualities and skills.

Good educational qualifications
Chemistry, maths and physics form the basis of chemical engineering and need to have been studied at an advanced level.

An open mind
Chemical engineers, especially those working in research, need to be open to change and prepared to adapt their ideas and accept new theories. This is because they cannot know for certain where their work will lead.

Careful record-keeping is vital This engineer is inspecting rows of chemical drums.

Patience
The answers to problems are not found overnight. Research can go on for years and may include long periods when very little progress is made.

Teamwork
Chemical engineers usually work in teams, sharing ideas and talking about their findings. They need to enjoy being part of a group.

The use of computers for organizing and analyzing data is essential in chemical engineering.

fact file

Chemical engineers need to take a degree in civil engineering before going on to study for professional examinations, which include both academic study and practical work. People wanting to become chemical engineers can take a modern apprenticeship, which involves work and study. Qualifications gained as a modern apprentice can lead to a place on a degree course.

Discipline

Chemical engineers need to approach their work in a methodical and organized way, keeping records up-to-date, noting details carefully and writing accurate reports. Working as part of a team means that everyone in the group must keep clear records and reports, which can be used by others as well as themselves.

Computer skills

Today, all engineering jobs involve the use of computers.

Language skills

Engineering projects are often international, which means speaking a foreign language is a great advantage to chemical engineers.

A day in the life of a chemical engineer

Amanda Leadbetter

Amanda is an engineer working in a chemical plant that produces alcohol for use in cleaning products.

8.30 am I arrive at my office, check through my emails and chat with the senior chemical engineer about the day's work. I receive a phone call from the operations leader telling me that the finished product is 'off spec', which means it doesn't match our customer's requirements.

9.00 am I rush to the chemical plant, change into my hard hat and overalls and meet the mechanical engineer, control engineer and senior operator to locate the source of the problem. This involves thinking on our feet and discussing why the problem is occurring! We need to work fast so the customer can receive the 'on-spec' material on time. The different parts of the plant are checked, including flow rates, temperatures and pressures. Eventually we find the problem, which is connected with the raw materials being used.

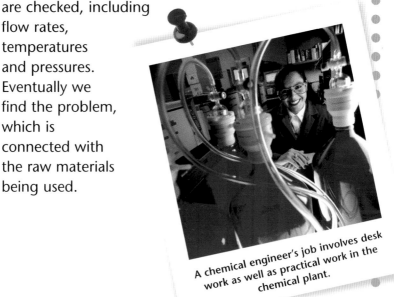

A chemical engineer's job involves desk work as well as practical work in the chemical plant.

In the chemical plant, workers consult the engineers' plans when problems arise.

10.30 am Problem solved! I settle down to some paperwork. Each month we produce figures showing the levels of waste gases and liquids given out into the atmosphere. These waste materials are reported to an external organization, which ensures we are not excessively polluting the environment.

12.30 pm Lunch, and a chance to chat with the team.

1.30 pm I prepare for a **teleconference** with the chemists based at our central research centre. We discuss future research plans to help us understand how to run the plant more efficiently, safely and in a cost-effective way.

4.00 pm Back at the chemical plant I check on the production process and chat with the operators to ensure that all is running safely and to our production plan.

5.00 pm Time to go home. With any luck, tomorrow will be quieter!

Civil Engineer

What is a civil engineer?

Civil engineers design and supervise the construction of the built environment needed by society. This includes water supply and sewerage networks, roads and railways, dams, tunnels, sports stadiums and bridges – in fact, the entire built environment you see around you and use every day. Life without civil engineers would be very uncomfortable and would soon become difficult and dangerous. Without civil engineers:

Civil engineers design large public buildings and make sure they are constructed properly. This sports stadium was built for the 2000 Olympic Games in Sydney, Australia.

- there would be no clean water available at the turn of a tap because water purification plants would not be built;

Dealing with disaster

Following a disaster such as a flood or an earthquake, civil engineers are as important as doctors. They set up water systems to provide clean drinking water and take dirty water away; they help rebuild bridges and roads and make sure buildings are safe.

Civil engineers design and supervise the building of dams to channel water for our use.

- the environment would suffer because dirty water would not wash away into sewers to be treated and re-used;
- new roads, railways and bridges would not be built;
- new buildings such as airports, railway stations and sports complexes would not be constructed;
- new homes would not be built;
- travel by air, road or rail would be almost impossible because transport systems would collapse;
- public health would suffer because diseases such as **cholera** and **dysentery** would soon spread, causing deadly **epidemics** and killing vast numbers of people.

Main tasks of a civil engineer

Civil engineers design building projects. They differ from architects in that their designs focus primarily on strength, safety and environmental concerns, from a scientific standpoint, and they are less concerned about the artistic aspects of architectural design.

- Coastal and marine civil engineers work in coastal areas, devising ways in which the land can be protected against flooding and **erosion**, and building marinas, harbours and ports.
- Civil engineers involved with environmental projects research ways of minimizing the effects of human activity on the environment. They design and install water and waste management systems for recycling water. They work to protect plants and

Railway systems are planned and created by civil engineers.

Good points and bad points

'No two days are ever the same, which is what I like best about my work as a civil engineer. I enjoy going out on site to see work in progress and structures being built from drawings.'

'Sometimes the work can be hectic, with several projects demanding my attention at the same time.'

animals by carrying out investigations into possible environmental damage that could be caused by engineering work.

● Civil engineers involved in facilities management examine the places where people work. Their function is to create safe and efficient working environments.

● Geotechnical civil engineers study the land on which a building is to be constructed and use this information to make sure the structure stands up and is safe.

● Civil engineers working on highways and bridges improve and rebuild existing roads and bridges and plan and supervise the building of new ones.

Other areas involving civil engineers include:

● power – working on energy projects such as wind farms, electricity plants or gasworks;

● rail transport – designing and building rail links, stations and depots;

● risk management – assessing the dangers, such as injury to employees or damage to the environment, before work begins on a project;

● construction – especially that of large structures such as multi-storey office and housing blocks, sports stadiums and airports;

● tunnel building – the construction of tunnels under rivers, mountains and the sea.

Here civil engineers supervise the construction of a bridge.

Skills needed to be a civil engineer

Good educational qualifications
Anyone wishing to become a civil engineer needs to have studied maths, physics and chemistry to a high level.

Computer skills
Today all engineering jobs involve the use of computers and much of the design work is carried out on-screen, using engineering design computer software packages.

Creativity
Civil engineers need to be able to imagine how something is going to look and consider the different ways in which it could be built.

Practicality
When they are designing and constructing a project, civil engineers need to understand how it can be built safely. They must also be aware of the different building methods involved and how the machinery works that is to be used during construction.

Constructing a tunnel beneath the sea between France and England was a huge engineering project. Here an engineer gives instructions to crane operators by walkie-talkie.

Many of the wonders of the modern world are designed by civil engineers.

Teamwork

Civil engineering projects are too large and complicated for one person to work on alone. Civil engineers are usually part of a team, sharing ideas and working closely with one another.

Management skills

Civil engineers need to know how to manage the design and construction of a project within a set price and time scale. They also need to know the information required by different groups involved in the work.

fact file

Civil engineers need to take a degree in civil engineering before going on to study for professional examinations, which include both academic study and practical work. People wanting to become civil engineers can take a modern apprenticeship, which involves work and study. Qualifications gained as a modern apprentice can lead to a place on a degree course.

A day in the life of a civil engineer

Karen Bridges

Karen is a senior engineer with a civil engineering consultancy which undertakes projects for clients ranging from building companies to public authorities. Karen has a degree and a professional qualification in civil engineering together with several years' experience.

8.30 am	I study a plan of a site and write a report on how to move different construction vehicles on to it.
9.30 am	I attend a meeting about a new project to decide on how to build a new theatre, what **ecology** needs protection and how people will travel to the site.
11.00 am	I give a talk to graduates about becoming professional engineers.
12.00 pm	I receive a phone call from a colleague on-site telling me that a crane cannot lift a beam into position. I look at some plans and do some calculations to try to solve the problem.
1.30 pm	I eat a sandwich while looking at a new project for a leisure centre which needs access for cars. I design the road and calculate the cost. I work hard, but I love my job. No two days are ever the same and I'm often involved in several projects at the same time.
2.15 pm	I meet with the client to discuss the building of the leisure centre.

3.30 pm I put on my hard hat and protective clothing and visit the site with the crane problem to see if my solution is working. It is, and construction work can continue.

4.00 pm I have a meeting with other representatives of companies working on a bridge project. I sketch ideas of what the bridge (over a river) would look like and we discuss how to build it.

6.00 pm I have a final cup of coffee and start designing the bridge. I am excited about how good this will look when it is built.

This civil engineer is using his specialist knowledge to work out how soon a volcano is likely to erupt. His findings should help protect people who live near the volcano.

Civil engineers work on-site to make sure a building is constructed properly.

weblinks

For more information about a career as a civil engineer, go to www.waylinks.co.uk/series/soyouwant/engineering

Electrical/Electronics Engineer

What is an electrical/electronics engineer?

Electronics engineers design and develop products that use electricity. These range from fun things, such as computer games, to items of medical equipment, such as heart monitors, which are used to save lives. Their work includes research and development, looking at ways of designing new pieces of equipment and improving existing ones.

Are the jobs of electrical engineer and electronics engineer the same? If not, what is the difference between them? The two jobs sound similar and, in some ways, they are. They are both closely connected with electricity, but there are some important differences between them.

This electrical engineer is working at the control centre of a company supplying electricity to millions of people.

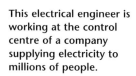

What is electricity?

Scientists have long known that electricity exists, and have discovered how to generate it on a large scale, but still find it difficult to explain exactly what it is.

A simple explanation is that electricity is a form of energy produced by the movement of **electrons**. There are two kinds of electricity: static electricity and current electricity. Static electricity such as lightning stays in one place. Current electricity is the flow of electric charge through a substance that conducts electricity, such as copper wire.

Electrical engineers are concerned mainly with generating or making electricity and supplying it to users, including offices, hospitals, schools, homes and factories. Without the knowledge and skill of electrical engineers, life as we live it today would be impossible.

Less than one hundred years ago, people would have found it hard to imagine themselves living in houses filled with equipment run by electricity. Yet today, washing machines, refrigerators, vacuum cleaners and computers are to be found in almost every home. These electrical items would not be there without the work of electronics engineers.

Electricity supplies are carried to places where they are needed via electrical distribution stations like this.

Main tasks of an electrical/electronics engineer

- Electrical engineers use different ways to generate, or make, electricity. These include making electricity from: fossil fuels, for example, coal, natural gas and **petroleum**, which are formed from the fossil remains of animals and plants; water (hydro-electric energy); and nuclear power.

- Electrical engineers research new ways of generating electricity, using renewable resources such as sun and wind.

- Electronics engineers design, develop, install and maintain a wide range of electrically driven products. They work in a variety of areas. Electronics engineers work on communications systems, sending information through **electromagnetic waves** via satellites. They work on new

Electricity is delivered via circuits, which need to be carefully drawn and constructed. This engineer is working on a blueprint of circuits on a lightbox.

Good points and bad points

'There are so many interesting jobs open to electronics engineers, for example, in research, design, installation and maintenance. The pay is good and so are the opportunities for promotion.'

'I do feel engineers need more recognition for the work they do in providing people with warm homes and good transport systems and in helping them keep fit and healthy.'

mobile phone technology that can send messages, pictures and video clips. They also work in the fields of robotics, developing robots to help humans by doing many tasks, and artificial intelligence, developing computers that may be capable of thinking for themselves.

- Electronics engineers are involved in microelectronics – making ever smaller electrical parts. The first computer weighed tons, but today a computer can fit inside a wristwatch. They are also employed in **nanotechnology**, designing machines no bigger than a speck of dust. These are of great use to medical science because in the future they could possibly be programmed to travel inside the body, fighting disease and repairing damage.

Electronics engineers are involved in the building of robotic arms, used in this picture to manufacture car parts.

- Electronics engineers work in the entertainment industry, building robotic models of humans, animals or fantasy creatures in a process called animatronics. The models are programmed to perform lifelike movements in time with a pre-recorded soundtrack and are used in television and film productions and in theme parks.

- Electronics engineers are also employed in health-care technology, where they design scanning and **ultrasound** equipment (to let doctors know what is happening inside a patient's body), electronic sensors and control systems to assist surgeons to carry out delicate surgery.

Skills needed to be an electrical/electronics engineer

Good educational qualifications
Anyone wishing to become an electrical or electronics engineer needs to have studied maths, physics and chemistry to a high level.

Computer skills
All engineering jobs involve computers, which are used for logging information, carrying out calculations and for design work using specialist software programmes.

An enquiring mind
Electrical and electronics engineers need to enjoy solving problems, answering questions and finding out how things work.

Creativity
Electrical and electronics engineers enjoy making things with their hands. At the same time they need to use their brains to work out why something works the way it does and whether it could be made in a better way.

Practicality
No matter how successful engineers become, they will always need to undertake practical work, examining parts of an engine or machine, and testing pieces of equipment to find out how a project is progressing.

Electrical engineers need to be interested in finding out how and why things work as they do. This engineer is making adjustments to **a transformer**.

Finding new ways of making electricity is vital for the future.

fact file

Electrical and electronics engineers need to take a degree in engineering before going on to study for professional examinations, which include both academic study and practical work. People wanting to become electrical and electronics engineers can take a modern apprenticeship, which involves work and study. Qualifications gained as a modern apprentice can lead to a place on a degree course.

Teamwork

Engineers do not work alone and keep their ideas to themselves. They need to get on well with other people, and enjoy sharing ideas and listening to what other members of the team have to say.

Communication skills

Engineers need to speak clearly and explain what they mean to people who do not have their high level of engineering knowledge.

Good colour vision

Electrical and electronics engineers need to be able to see all colours accurately, because electric wires are identified by their colours.

14152

A day in the life of an electronics engineer

Vivien Lang

Vivien is a senior engineer with a major car manufacturer. She has a degree in electrical engineering with electronics, and joined the company when she left university.

I head a team of ten engineers working on the research and development of in-car telephones, radios and navigation equipment.

9.00 am I take part in a team meeting to discuss the progress being made in different areas of our work. We deal with customer issues as well as designing and developing new equipment. If a customer is not satisfied with the electrical equipment in a car, the problem is passed to us.

10.30 am I take a look at the projects the team is working on. There are three ways in which we carry out tests. Firstly we test the equipment on a workbench in the laboratory. Next we test it on what is known as a breadboard – a lab car without a **chassis** or wheels. After tests have been completed, the equipment is fitted into a car for the final stage, when everything is tested to make sure there are no problems.

12.30 pm Back at my desk, I catch up with some phone calls and check my emails.

2.00 pm After lunch, I check my notes before heading for a meeting. Today people want a great deal from their cars and I'm attending a meeting with senior staff in the company, looking at ways in which customer needs can be met in the future.

5.00 pm A lot of good ideas have come out of the meeting and people are still discussing them.

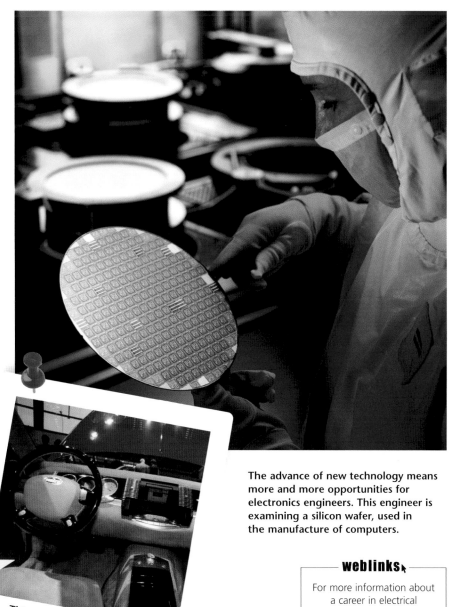

This expensive new car has a computerized dashboard, built with the help of electronics engineers.

The advance of new technology means more and more opportunities for electronics engineers. This engineer is examining a silicon wafer, used in the manufacture of computers.

weblinks

For more information about a career in electrical engineering, go to www.waylinks.co.uk/series/soyouwant/engineering

Manufacturing Engineer

What is a manufacturing engineer?

Manufacturing engineers organize ways of changing raw materials into manufactured products. Their work often covers a number of different engineering disciplines, such as mechanical and electrical engineering. What do cars, cans, biscuits and boats have in common? The answer is that they would not exist without the work of manufacturing engineers.

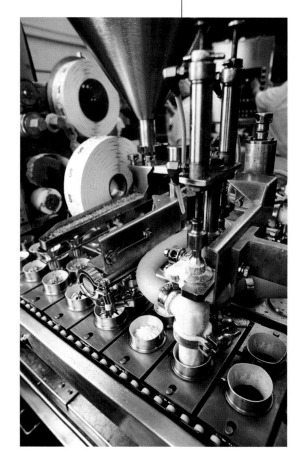

This ice-cream production plant involves machines with lots of moving parts. Manufacturing engineers make sure that machines like this run smoothly.

Manufacturing engineers can be found in a wide range of industries, including the production of cars, agricultural equipment, **pharmaceuticals** and food. Although their work includes administration duties such as writing reports and analyzing material, manufacturing engineers usually spend only a small amount of their working day sitting at a desk. Usually they are to be found in the production areas where the goods are made, talking to the people who operate the machines and checking that the machinery is working well. Manufacturing

The canning process

In 1795, Emperor Napoleon of France offered a prize to the person who could think of the best way of preserving food for the French army. An inventor, Nicholas Appert, came up with the idea for the canning process. In this way, one of the world's largest manufacturing industries was born. Today, most homes have some tinned food on the kitchen shelves.

This manufacturing engineer is checking a computer print-out of pharmaceutical products.

engineers also report back on production matters to management groups in the company.

Manufacturing engineers are always looking for ways to improve production, considering how:

- systems can be made to run more quickly and efficiently;
- money can be saved in making the product;
- the quality of the product can be improved;
- the manufacturing process can be made as safe as possible.

Main tasks of a manufacturing engineer

Manufacturing engineers need to carry out a lot of research to make sure their company buys the best possible equipment for the job. New machinery is a big investment, so before any money is spent on it manufacturing engineers need to discuss with colleagues exactly what they want it to do. They also carry out their own research in order to find out:

- the job the machinery will do;
- how it should fit in with existing machinery;
- how much money there is available to spend;
- when the equipment is needed.

When the research work is complete, a report is written, outlining possible alternatives. These could include designing equipment to meet the company's requirements or buying equipment and adapting it to do a particular job. It is the manufacturing engineer's responsibility to design equipment and plan its uses.

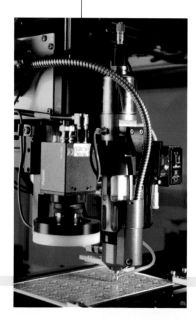

New manufacturing equipment, like this automated machine for assembling computer chips, costs a great deal of money.

Good points and bad points

'There's a lot of satisfaction to be gained from running an efficient production area.'

'Sometimes people expect me to be able to work miracles by repairing a machine or installing new equipment in an impossibly short space of time.'

An engineer at
work in a factory
producing
hydraulic test
equipment.

In a manufacturing situation, machinery is usually
part of a production line. This means that each piece
of equipment should work with other machinery so
that the production process runs smoothly.
Manufacturing engineers supervise the installation
(putting in) of new machinery. They then organize
trial runs of the new equipment during which they
can identify and put right any problems.

Manufacturing engineers organize regular maintenance
checks to make sure equipment is running properly
and safely. Machinery breaks down even in the most
efficiently run factory. Breakdowns can be expensive
because money is lost when goods are not produced.
It is the responsibility of the manufacturing engineer to
see that problems are put right as quickly as possible.

Skills needed to be a manufacturing engineer

Manufacturing engineers may find themselves under pressure from colleagues who want problems put right immediately. In order to do their job well, manufacturing engineers need a wide range of skills.

Good educational qualifications
Anyone wishing to become a manufacturing engineer needs a very high level of technical knowledge. Qualifications in maths and science subjects (particularly physics) are essential.

Computer skills
Manufacturing engineers use computers for many tasks, including designing machinery, storing information and writing reports.

Problem-solving skills
Manufacturing engineers need to deal with emergencies, such as the breakdown of machinery, on a regular basis. They must be able to think calmly and logically for solutions to a problematic situation.

Manufacturing engineers may be called in to deal with problems, as on this washing machine assembly line.

Practicality
Manufacturing engineers work in a hands-on way with factory equipment. They need to use their practical skills to work on machinery, as well as understanding the theory of how it works.

Communication skills
Manufacturing engineers come into contact with many people, from machine operators to company directors, and have to be able to talk to all of them.

The bottled water on this conveyor belt will soon be for sale in the shops.

They also need to explain technical matters to people who do not have their level of technical knowledge.

Tact
Sometimes manufacturing engineers have to inform colleagues of news they don't want to hear, for example, that a piece of equipment is going to cost a great deal to repair or that a problem is not going to be solved easily.

Health and safety
Manufacturing areas can be dangerous places and manufacturing engineers need to be aware of this and to work with caution and care.

Teamwork
Manufacturing engineers need to enjoy being part of a team, working closely with other people and sharing ideas.

Matthew Clubb

Matthew works as a manufacturing engineer for a small company which makes drilling tools for use in drilling operations across the world.

9.00 am I am putting together a quote for a drilling tool to be used on an offshore oil rig. This includes finding out the cost of different materials and estimating the number of hours it will take to complete the job. It's quite tricky and I can't afford to make a mistake.

11.00 am I'm at my computer designing some tools to be used by a client in the oil industry. Using computer-aided design software, I can create a **three dimensional** drawing on screen. The design is very detailed and has to be correct to thousandths of an inch.

1.00 pm Lunch consists of a sandwich and a cup of coffee. The firm I work for is very small and doesn't run to facilities such as a canteen. It is also the reason why I am involved in all aspects of the company's work

2.00 pm I send some designs to clients via the Internet, using a password protected system which only they can open.

Manufacturing engineers design drilling tools used on rigs to extract oil from the sea bed.

Operatives **weld** sections of heavy machinery together in the machine shop.

3.00 pm My clients have now had a chance to examine the designs so they phone to talk over any changes they feel need to be made.

3.30 pm I'm in the machine shop talking to one of the operatives who turns my designs into reality. Five operatives work here and we keep in close contact, so that they can see the wider process as well as their own part of the work.

4.15 pm I'm back at my desk. Answers to some of my questions have come through, so I can move this morning's quote on further.

5.00 pm Everything is on schedule, so we can close down for the night. There have been occasions when all of us have worked over the weekend in the machine shop to finish a job on time.

Marine Engineer

What is a marine engineer?

Marine engineers are responsible for designing, building and repairing ships and sailing craft so that they are sea-worthy and able to cope with fierce storms and long periods of time in the water.

Marine engineers design exploration vehicles, such as these underwater scooters.

The sea covers 70 per cent of the earth's surface. It has played an important part in world trade for hundreds of years. Marine engineers make it possible for us to use the oceans' resources. However, they also play an important environmental role, working to make sure that people do not damage sea life.

The sinking of the Titanic

When it was built, the *Titanic* was the largest ship ever made and was thought to be unsinkable. On the fourth night of its maiden voyage in 1912, a lookout in the **crow's nest** spotted an iceberg ahead. The ship tried to turn but crashed into the iceberg. The number of lifeboats was limited and, although 705 lives were saved, 1,502 passengers and crew drowned.

Although the shipbuilding industry has declined in recent times, the number of leisure craft, such as luxury sailing yachts, has increased. Leisure craft tend to be bought by wealthy people, and this has provided new employment for marine engineers.

The work of marine engineers has also grown with the discovery of precious resources, such as oil and gas, under the sea. Marine engineers look into ways of locating these resources, extracting them and transporting them to dry land. To this end, they design off-shore drilling platforms. They have also developed instruments that can explore areas of the ocean which were previously out of human reach.

Most international cargo is carried by sea.

Main tasks of a marine engineer

There are three main branches of marine engineering:

- *Ocean engineering – working beneath the sea*
This involves exploring the seabed for substances such as oil, gas and minerals, using remote control instruments to explore the seabed, and developing environmentally friendly ways of disposing of machinery and equipment in the sea when they are no longer needed.

This marine engineer is inputting data on a laptop on board ship.

- *Offshore engineering – working at sea*
This involves designing, operating and maintaining off-shore platforms and systems used to extract materials from the sea. It includes finding ways to overcome problems caused by bad weather conditions and rough seas. Marine engineers work on board ships such as

Good points and bad points

'As a marine engineer I spend long periods of time working at sea. This means that I have managed to see quite a lot of the world in a short time. I have also learnt to make decisions for myself, which is important because I'm the only engineer on board.'

'I did find being away from family and friends for months at a time difficult at first, and I still find myself feeling slightly homesick on dates like my birthday or at Christmas.'

Marine engineers
also design
leisure boats and
competition
craft. Here a
boat designer
discusses his
plans with the
ship's captain.

cruise liners, cargo ships and pipe-laying vessels, making sure the engines, equipment and systems are running properly.

● *Onshore engineering – working on dry land*
This involves shipbuilding and ship repair. There are still good openings for marine engineers in the building of specialist vessels such as pipe-laying ships, tankers, survey ships and leisure boats. Marine engineers are also involved in the design and manufacturing of specialized equipment for boats. Marine insurance companies employ marine engineers to check that the ships they insure are well designed, properly built and kept in good condition. Marine engineers work for coastguard agencies, checking marine safety, and preventing and dealing with pollution.

Many marine engineers travel to different parts of the world as part of their job, working in areas such as the Pacific Rim, the Middle East and the South Atlantic. There are good opportunities for marine engineers in the navy and in civilian life.

Skills needed to be a marine engineer

Love of the sea
Marine engineers need to have a real fascination for and interest in the sea. As in all areas of engineering, change happens fast and they need to keep up with new developments across the world.

Good educational qualifications
Anyone wishing to become a marine engineer needs a very high level of knowledge in maths, physics, chemistry and biology.

French marine engineer, Alain Thébault, has designed a specialized high-speed sailboat. He is shown here at its launch at the Paris Boat Show.

Eye for detail
The sea can be unpredictable and dangerous. Marine engineers must consider all sorts of possibilities in their designs and make sure they are correct to the smallest detail.

Quick thinking
Even with the most careful planning, problems do arise. Marine engineers must deal with these calmly and efficiently to prevent a disaster developing.

Practicality
Many marine engineering jobs involve working on-site, at sea, under the sea, or at the coast. Marine engineers need to enjoy getting out and about and working on projects. There are excellent travel opportunities for people wishing to work abroad.

Teamwork

Marine engineering projects usually involve a number of people, including engineers, scientists and divers, all working as part of a group. They need to be able to work together and share ideas.

An easygoing personality

Marine engineers can spend long periods at sea, working and socializing with the same small group of people, so they need to get on well with others and to enjoy their own company as well.

Computer skills

All engineering jobs involve the use of computers for different jobs, including design work, calculations, report-writing and record-keeping.

fact file

Marine engineers need to take a degree in marine engineering or a similar subject before going on to further study and practical experience. People wanting to become marine engineers can take a modern apprenticeship, which involves work and study. Qualifications gained as a modern apprentice can lead to a place on a degree course.

Some marine engineers have diving qualifications and are able to check projects under the sea for themselves.

Anna Evangelidis

Anna is a marine engineer with an offshore pipeline construction company. She currently works on a vessel that is laying pipelines to carry oil and gas from the North Sea.

6.30 am   We work a twelve-hour shift, from 7.00 am to 7.00 pm seven days a week, so it's an early start. Engineers spend six weeks at a time at sea. I have my own cabin, which gives me some privacy.

7.15 am   I'm one of two marine engineers on board. Our job is to supervise the laying of the pipeline and make sure it falls in the right place. The sections of pipe are welded together on board ship and then dropped off the back into the sea, rather like a long sausage.

Computerized calculations mean we know exactly how and where to drop the pipe to get it in the right position. Divers attach the pipe to the platform; they work from a specialized boat called a dive support vessel.

Marine engineers spend several weeks at a time working on board ship.

weblinks

For more information about a career in marine engineering, go to
www.waylinks.co.uk/series/
soyouwant/engineering

This marine engineer is running a test on submarine equipment.

9.30 am   It's time to eat. The food is very good on board, so it's easy to put on weight.

10.00 am   Back to work. I've been on board for a month and am on good terms with the welding team.

2.00 pm   All is going well until difficulties arise with the welding equipment. The welding is not up to standard, which means it is likely to crack and leak oil into the ocean. We need to lay a set length of piping each day and now it looks as though we won't meet our target.

3.30 pm   All we can do is wait while the welders solve the problem. Tests show that they have put matters right, so we set to work to make up for lost time.

7.00 pm   I've finished for the day. There's a gym on board, but I'm so tired I'm going to shower, eat and go to bed.

Mechanical Engineer

What is a mechanical engineer?

Mechanical engineers work with anything that moves in a mechanical way, including the moving parts of engines, such as gears and pulleys. They also work with substances such as air, oil and water, which can be moved mechanically. If an object is manufactured, a mechanical engineer will have been involved in its development.

The responsibilities of mechanical engineers are very varied. They work closely with other engineers and sometimes overlap with other fields of engineering. The work of mechanical engineers is divided into different areas. Medical engineering uses the principles

Mechanical engineers work on machines with moving parts, like these metal gears.

The steam engine

Thomas Newcomen lived between 1663 and 1729 and was the inventor of the steam engine. However, this invention is usually credited to James Watt, a Scottish engineer, who carried out improvements on the original design.

Newcomen's invention was widely used in mines, where it was operated to drain water from underground tunnels at a much deeper level than had been possible before. This increased the amount of coal and iron that could be mined.

of mechanical engineering to design, test and develop equipment to improve human health. Automotive engineering is the design and development of land-based vehicles such as cars, trucks and motorcycles.

The first steam engine, designed by James Watt, is world famous.

Railway engineering falls into two parts: traction and rolling stock engineering – working on the development of trains, coaches and wagons; and infrastructure engineering – working on tracks, signs and power supplies. Sports engineering involves researching and designing equipment used by athletes.

In the field of renewable energy engineering, mechanical, electrical, civil and chemical engineers are involved in finding new ways to convert renewable energy sources such as wind, water and sunlight into electricity for homes and businesses.

Main tasks of a mechanical engineer

The work of mechanical engineers includes:

- design – deciding how a machine is to work and drawing up plans to achieve this;
- development – making the plans a reality by building the machine;
- testing – running the machine under different conditions to discover problems and put them right;
- installation – fitting the machine into place in a factory or the environment in which it is to work, making sure that it operates successfully with other pieces of equipment and machinery;
- operation – carrying out regular checks to make sure the machinery is working properly;
- maintenance and repair – keeping the machinery in good order, dealing with any problems that occur and supervising maintenance staff.

This medical engineer is working on a new type of syringe.

Good points and bad points

'I have always wanted a job which absorbs me and keeps me on my toes. Working in research is both exciting and interesting and nothing beats the feeling of satisfaction gained from making progress in a project.'

'The work is painstaking and there are long periods when, despite my best efforts, I don't seem to be getting very far.'

Medical engineering includes working on **prosthetics** or artificial limbs that are comfortable and can grip and hold objects, and developing mechanical hearts, replacement kidneys and **diagnostic** equipment such as **x-rays** and ultrasound. Mechanical engineers also work on **nanorobots** that travel through the human body and repair damaged **arteries**.

Automotive engineering includes improving seatbelt systems, developing better security systems to fight crime, reducing the cost of manufacturing vehicle parts and running **corrosion** tests to combat rusting. Automotive engineers also work on the development of environmentally friendly car engines that run on alternatives to petrol.

Sports engineering includes developing training shoes that measure the slipperiness of the ground beneath them and examining the technology behind skateboard, snowboard and ski design.

Sports engineers work on designs which will lead to improved equipment for athletes.

Skills needed to be a mechanical engineer

Good educational qualifications
People wanting to become mechanical engineers should study maths and science subjects at school.

Computer skills
All engineering jobs involve the use of computers.

Problem-solving
Mechanical engineers should gain enjoyment and satisfaction from developing solutions to problems and deciding which solution works best.

Computer-aided design gives mechanical engineers the flexibility to change their plans quickly and easily.

Quick-thinking
Mechanical engineers need to be able to think on their feet. They have to work out ways of dealing with problems as speedily as possible. This is especially true for those who are working in production, dealing with equipment in factories or in manufacturing areas.

Creativity
Mechanical engineers need to be able to imagine how something is going to work and consider the different ways in which it could be built.

weblinks

For more information about a career in mechanical engineering, go to www.waylinks.co.uk/series/soyouwant/engineering

Mechanical engineers inspect a generator at a power plant.

Practicality

Mechanical engineers need to have an organized approach to their work because they must aim to set budgets and finish projects within a certain time.

Flexibility

Mechanical engineers need to see when their ideas aren't working and change them when necessary.

Teamwork

Engineers are involved in practical projects. They need to share ideas and work well as part of a group.

fact file

Mechanical engineers need to take a degree in mechanical engineering and then work towards professional status through practical experience and further study. People wanting to become mechanical engineers can take a modern apprenticeship, which involves work and study. Qualifications gained as a modern apprentice can lead to a place on a degree course.

A day in the life of a mechanical engineer

Peter Davis

Peter works as a mechanical engineer for a car production company. He designs exterior trim parts for cars.

9.00 am   I've been fascinated by cars since I was a child, so being part of the design team working on new models is about as exciting as it gets for me. My job involves designing the parts that are attached to the exterior of a car. They include badges, bumpers and body side mouldings.

Using a computer-aided design programme, I begin work on a new body trim for a sports car that the company is planning to launch. I have to keep several points in mind while doing this, including the overall look of the car.

11.00 am   I attend a meeting where we are given details of a new project – the possible launch of a family car with a sporty look. It sounds really exciting and I can't wait to get started!

1.00 pm   The meeting extends into lunch as everybody wants to talk about the new idea.

Computers are used widely in most areas of car design and production.

1.45 pm   Back to reality: I've been running some initial tests on bumpers I've designed. The tests are to make sure that the bumpers are strong enough to protect the body of the car. I check the results, which are good, but there are still a lot more tests to be carried out before I can be confident that my design is ready for production.

3.00 pm   I begin work on a detailed analysis of the results of the bumper tests.

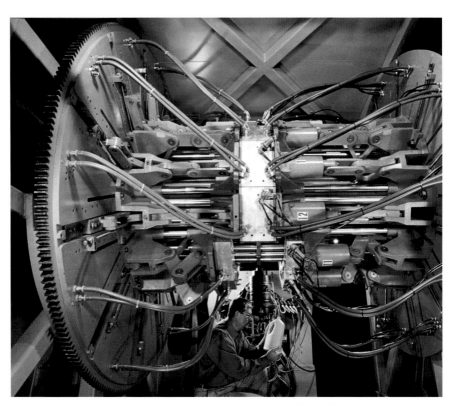

Mechanical engineers need to run regular maintenance checks of machinery. In this photo, an engineer inspects plastic processing machinery.

14452

Glossary

antibiotics – substances that are able to kill bacteria in the body or make them harmless.

arteries – blood vessels carrying blood from the heart to other parts of the body.

automated flight control – flying a plane using a computerized system instead of a human pilot.

automotive – involving motor vehicles.

chassis – the frame and wheels that support the engine and body of a motor vehicle.

cholera – a serious disease, often fatal, caused by swallowing contaminated food or water.

civilian – someone who is an ordinary citizen and not a member of the armed forces.

corrosion – the destruction of metal by a chemical action, for example, the rusting of iron.

crow's nest – a lookout point at the top of a ship's mast.

delegate – a person chosen to represent a company, for example, at a conference.

diagnostic – the identification of an illness or medical condition.

dysentery – a serious illness caused by bacteria in the lower intestine and resulting in severe diarrhoea.

ecology – the study of relationships between living things and the environment in which they live.

electromagnetic waves – electromagnetism is magnetism produced by electric currents. Electromagnetic waves are surges of energy within electromagnetic fields.

electrons – tiny particles that orbit the nucleus, or centre, of an atom. An atom is the smallest quantity of an element that can take part in a chemical reaction.

environment – the external surroundings in which people, plants or animals live.

epidemics – outbreaks of disease which spread quickly among groups of people.

erosion – the wearing away of rock or soil.

hydraulic – describes something operated by pressure transmitted through a pipe by a liquid.

manufacture – to make a product on a large scale by industrial processes.

modifications – changes, improvements.

nanorobots – tiny robots.

nanotechnology – the science of designing tiny machines.

petroleum – crude oil.

pharmaceuticals – the production and sale of drugs used in medicine.

plastic – a type of synthetic material that can be moulded when soft, then set into a shape.

prosthetics – designing and making artificial body parts.

simulation – the act of reproducing a situation, often for training purposes. For example, simulated flights are used to teach trainee pilots how to fly, before they actually go up in the air in an aircraft themselves.

synthetics – materials made artificially by chemical reaction.

teleconference – a meeting held between people in different places, making contact through telecommunications equipment such as phones and video links.

three dimensional – possessing both height, width and depth.

transformer – a machine that transfers a current from one circuit to one or more other circuits.

ultrasound – an imaging technique using high frequency sound waves.

weld – to fix pieces of metal or plastic together, usually by heating.

x-ray – an image produced by passing high energy electromagnetic radiation through the body.

Further Information

So do you still want to work in engineering?

This book does not aim to cover every job in the engineering industry, but it should give you a taste of what engineering is about. It is a practical profession and offers exciting opportunities to make a real contribution to the future.

What this book does hope to do is to give you an idea of the range of different jobs, and what working in them is really like. Although it covers different types of engineering, the future of engineering is likely to lead to multi-skilling. This means that tomorrow's engineers will often work in more than one engineering area. This is particularly true of mechanical and electronic engineering, where engineers work on electronic equipment that has mechanical parts.

If you are at secondary school and seriously interested in a career in engineering, ask your careers teacher if he or she could arrange for some work experience.

A word of warning if you are considering becoming an engineer. Choose the subjects you study at school or college with care and make sure these will lead to an engineering career. The names of some subjects can be misleading. For example, the term 'design engineer' suggests that it is closely linked to graphics and art. In fact, it is a specialist engineering area and requires a high level of knowledge in maths and science.

Books

If you want to find out more about working in the engineering industry, you will find the following helpful:

Real People Working in Building and Construction, written by Blythe Camenson, published by Contemporary Books, 1999.

Working in Electrical and Electronic Engineering, published by Careers and Occupational Information Centre.

Working in Engineering, published by Careers and Occupational Information Centre, 1999.

Q & A: Studying Chemical Engineering, published by Trotman, 2000.

weblinks

For more engineering careers advice, go to www.waylinks.co.uk/series/soyouwant/engineering

Useful addresses

United Kingdom

Engineering Council UK
10 Maltravers Street
London
WC2R 3ER
Tel: 020 7240 7891

Institution of Chemical
Engineers
Davis Building
165-189 Railway Terrace
Rugby
CV21 3HQ
Tel: 01788 534459

Institution of Civil
Engineers
1 Great George Street
London
SW1P 3AA
Tel: 020 7222 7722

Institution of Electrical
Engineers
Savoy Place
London
WC2R 0BL
Tel: 020 7240 1871

Institution of Incorporated
Engineers
Savoy Hill House
Savoy Hill
London
WC2R 0BS
Tel: 020 7836 3357

Institute of Marine
Engineering, Science and
Technology
80 Coleman Street
London
EC2R 5BJ
Tel: 020 7382 2600

Institution of Mechanical
Engineers
1 Birdcage Walk
London
SW1H 9JJ
Tel: 020 7222 7899

SEMTA
(Sector Skills Council for
Science, Engineering and
Manufacturing
Technologies)
14 Upton Road
Watford
Herts
WD18 0JT
Tel: 0800 282167

SEMTA Scotland
105 West George Street
Glasgow
G2 1QL
Tel: 0141 847 0977

Society of Environmental
Engineers
The Manor House
High Street
Buntingford
Herts
SG9 9AB
Tel: 01763 271209

The Year in Industry
The Simon Building
University of Manchester
Oxford Road
Manchester
M13 9PL
Tel: 0161 278 2497

Australia

Institution of Engineers
Australia
www.ieaust.org.au

New Zealand

Institution of Professional
Engineers New Zealand
Molesworth House
101 Molesworth Street
Wellington
New Zealand
Tel: +64 4473 9444

South Africa

Engineering Council of
South Africa
Private Bag X691
BRUMA 2026
Johannesburg
Tel (011) 607 9500

Index